THE HOUND OF HEAVEN

THE HOUND
OF HEAVEN

AND OTHER POEMS

BY

FRANCIS THOMPSON

FLEMING H. REVELL COMPANY
WESTWOOD · NEW JERSEY

DEDICATION OF *POEMS*

(1893)

To Wilfrid and Alice Meynell

IF the rose in meek duty
    May dedicate humbly
To her grower the beauty
    Wherewith she is comely;
If the mine to the miner
    The jewels that pined in it,
Earth to diviner
    The springs he divined in it;
To the grapes the wine-pitcher
    Their juice that was crushed in it,
Viol to its witcher
    The music lay hushed in it;
If the lips may pay Gladness
    In laughters she wakened,
And the heart to its sadness
    Weeping unslakened,
If the hid and sealed coffer,
    Whose having not his is,
To the loosers may proffer
    Their finding—here this is;

Their lives if all livers
　　　To the Life of all living,—
To you, O dear givers!
　　　I give your own giving.

CONTENTS

THE HOUND OF HEAVEN

THE HOUND OF HEAVEN

I FLED Him, down the nights and down the days;
  I fled Him, down the arches of the years;
I fled Him, down the labyrinthine ways
   Of my own mind; and in the mist of tears
I hid from Him, and under running laughter.
            Up vistaed hopes I sped;
            And shot, precipitated,
Adown Titanic glooms of chasmed fears,
   From those strong Feet that followed, followed after.
            But with unhurrying chase,
            And unperturbèd pace,
      Deliberate speed, majestic instancy,
            They beat—and a Voice beat
            More instant than the Feet—
      "All things betray thee, who betrayest Me."

            I pleaded, outlaw-wise,
By many a hearted casement, curtained red,
   Trellised with intertwining charities;
(For, though I knew His love Who followèd,
            Yet was I sore adread
Lest, having Him, I must have naught beside)

But, if one little casement parted wide,
    The gust of His approach would clash it to:
    Fear wist not to evade, as Love wist to pursue.
Across the margent of the world I fled,
    And troubled the gold gateways of the stars,
    Smiting for shelter on their clangèd bars;
        Fretted to dulcet jars
And silvern chatter the pale ports o' the moon.
I said to Dawn: Be sudden—to Eve: Be soon;
    With thy young skiey blossoms heap me over
        From this tremendous Lover—
Float thy vague veil about me, lest He see!
    I tempted all His servitors, but to find
My own betrayal in their constancy,
In faith to Him their fickleness to me,
    Their traitorous trueness, and their loyal deceit.
To all swift things for swiftness did I sue;
    Clung to the whistling mane of every wind.
        But whether they swept, smoothly fleet,
        The long savannahs of the blue;
            Or whether, Thunder-driven,
        They clanged his chariot 'thwart a heaven,
Plashy with flying lightnings round the spurn
        o' their feet:—
    Fear wist not to evade as Love wist to pursue.
        Still with unhurrying chase,

And unperturbèd pace,
Deliberate speed, majestic instancy,
Came on the following Feet,
And a Voice about their beat—
"Naught shelters thee, who wilt not shelter Me."

I sought no more that after which I strayed
In face of man or maid;
But still within the little children's eyes
Seems something, something that replies,
They at least are for me, surely for me!
I turned me to them very wistfully;
But just as their young eyes grew sudden fair
With dawning answers there,
Their angel plucked them from me by the hair.
"Come then, ye other children, Nature's—share
With me" (said I) "your delicate fellowship;
Let me greet you lip to lip,
Let me twine with you caresses,
Wantoning
With our Lady-Mother's vagrant tresses,
Banqueting
With her in her wind-walled palace,
Underneath her azured daïs,
Quaffing, as your taintless way is,
From a chalice

Lucent-weeping out of the dayspring."
        So it was done:
I in their delicate fellowship was one—
Drew the bolt of Nature's secrecies.
        I knew all the swift importings
        On the wilful face of skies;
        I knew how the clouds arise
        Spumèd of the wild sea-snortings;
          All that's born or dies
          Rose and drooped with; made them shapers
Of mine own moods, or wailful or divine;
        With them joyed and was bereaven.
        I was heavy with the even,
        When she lit her glimmering tapers
        Round the day's dead sanctities.
        I laughed in the morning's eyes.
I triumphed and I saddened with all weather,
        Heaven and I wept together,
And its sweet tears were salt with mortal mine;
Against the red throb of its sunset-heart
        I laid my own to beat,
        And share commingling heat;
But not by that, by that, was eased my human smart,
In vain my tears were wet on Heaven's grey cheek.
For ah! we know not what each other says,
        These things and I; in sound *I* speak—

Their sound is but their stir, they speak by silences.
Nature, poor stepdame, cannot slake my drouth;
      Let her, if she would owe me,
Drop yon blue bosom-veil of sky, and show me
      The breasts o' her tenderness:
Never did any milk of hers once bless
        My thirsting mouth.
        Nigh and nigh draws the chase,
        With unperturbèd pace,
     Deliberate speed, majestic instancy;
        And past those noisèd Feet
        A Voice comes yet more fleet—
    "Lo! naught contents thee, who content'st not
      Me."

Naked I wait Thy love's uplifted stroke!
My harness piece by piece Thou hast hewn from me,
      And smitten me to my knee;
     I am defenceless utterly.
     I slept, methinks, and woke,
And, slowly gazing, find me stripped in sleep.
In the rash lustihead of my young powers,
      I shook the pillaring hours
And pulled my life upon me; grimed with smears,
I stand amid the dust o' the mounded years—
My mangled youth lies dead beneath the heap.

My days have crackled and gone up in smoke,
Have puffed and burst as sun-starts on a stream.
　　　Yea, faileth now even dream
The dreamer, and the lute the lutanist;
Even the linked fantasies, in whose blossomy twist
I swung the earth a trinket at my wrist,
Are yielding; cords of all too weak account
For earth with heavy griefs so overplussed.
　　　Ah! is Thy love indeed
A weed, albeit an amaranthine weed,
Suffering no flowers except its own to mount?
　　　Ah! must—
　　　Designer infinite!—
Ah! must Thou char the wood ere Thou canst
　　　limn with it?
My freshness spent its wavering shower i' the dust;
And now my heart is as a broken fount,
Wherein tear-drippings stagnate, spilt down ever
　　　From the dank thoughts that shiver
Upon the sightful branches of my mind.
　　　Such is; what is to be?
The pulp so bitter, how shall taste the rind?
I dimly guess what Time in mists confounds;
Yet ever and anon a trumpet sounds
From the hid battlements of Eternity;
Those shaken mists a space unsettle, then

Round the half-glimpsèd turrets slowly wash again.
But not ere him who summoneth
I first have seen, enwound
With glooming robes purpureal, cypress-crowned;
His name I know, and what his trumpet saith.
Whether man's heart or life it be which yields
Thee harvest, must Thy harvest-fields
Be dunged with rotten death?

Now of that long pursuit
Comes on at hand the bruit;
That Voice is round me like a bursting sea:
"And is thy earth so marred,
Shattered in shard on shard?
Lo, all things fly thee, for thou fliest Me!

"Strange, piteous, futile thing!
Wherefore should any set thee love apart?
Seeing none but I makes much of naught" (He said),
"And human love needs human meriting:
How hast thou merited—
Of all man's clotted clay the dingiest clot?
Alack, thou knowest not
How little worthy of any love thou art!
Whom wilt thou find to love ignoble thee,
Save Me, save only Me?

All which I took from thee I did but take,
　　　　Not for thy harms,
But just that thou might'st seek it in My arms.
　　　　All which thy child's mistake
Fancies as lost, I have stored for thee at home:
　　　　Rise, clasp My hand, and come!"

　　Halts by me that footfall:
　　Is my gloom, after all,
Shade of His hand, outstretched caressingly?
　　"Ah, fondest, blindest, weakest,
　　I am He Whom thou seekest!
Thou dravest love from thee, who dravest Me."

HEAVEN AND HELL

'TIS said there were no thought of hell,
  Save hell were taught; that there should be
A Heaven for all's self-credible.
  Not so the thing appears to me.
'Tis Heaven that lies beyond our sights,
  And hell too possible that proves;
For all can feel the God that smites,
  But ah, how few the God that loves!

THE KINGDOM OF GOD

'In no Strange Land'

O WORLD invisible, we view thee,
  O world intangible, we touch thee,
O world unknowable, we know thee,
Inapprehensible, we clutch thee!

Does the fish soar to find the ocean,
The eagle plunge to find the air—
That we ask of the stars in motion
If they have rumour of thee there?

Not where the wheeling systems darken,
And our benumbed conceiving soars!—
The drift of pinions, would we hearken,
Beats at our own clay-shuttered doors.

The angels keep their ancient places;—
Turn but a stone, and start a wing!
'Tis ye, 'tis your estrangèd faces,
That miss the many-splendoured thing.

But (when so sad thou canst not sadder)
Cry;—and upon thy so sore loss
Shall shine the traffic of Jacob's ladder
Pitched betwixt Heaven and Charing Cross.

Yea, in the night, my Soul, my daughter,
Cry,—clinging Heaven by the hems;
And lo, Christ walking on the water
Not of Gennesareth, but Thames!

LOVE AND THE CHILD

"WHY do you so clasp me,
    And draw me to your knee?
Forsooth, you do but chafe me,
    I pray you let me be:
I will be loved but now and then
    When it liketh me!"

So I heard a young child,
    A thwart child, a young child
Rebellious against love's arms,
    Make its peevish cry.

To the tender God I turn:—
    "Pardon, Love most High!
For I think those arms were even Thine,
    And that child even I."

LITTLE JESUS

*Ex ore infantium, Deus, et lactentium
perfecisti laudem*

LITTLE Jesus, wast Thou shy
Once, and just so small as I?
And what did it feel like to be
Out of Heaven, and just like me?
Didst Thou sometimes think of *there*,
And ask where all the angels were?
I should think that I would cry
For my house all made of sky;
I would look about the air,
And wonder where my angels were;
And at waking 'twould distress me—
Not an angel there to dress me!
Hadst Thou ever any toys,
Like us little girls and boys?
And didst Thou play in Heaven with all
The angels that were not too tall,
With stars for marbles? Did the things
Play *Can you see me?* through their wings?
And did Thy Mother let Thee spoil
Thy robes, with playing on *our* soil?

How nice to have them always new
In Heaven, because 'twas quite clean blue!

Didst Thou kneel at night to pray,
And didst Thou join Thy hands, this way?
And did they tire sometimes, being young,
And make the prayer seem very long?
And dost Thou like it best, that we
Should join our hands to pray to Thee?

I used to think, before I knew,
The prayer not said unless we do.
And did Thy Mother at the night
Kiss Thee, and fold the clothes in right?
And didst Thou feel quite good in bed,
Kissed, and sweet, and Thy prayers said?

Thou canst not have forgotten all
That it feels like to be small:
And Thou know'st I cannot pray
To Thee in my father's way—
When Thou wast so little, say,
Couldst Thou talk Thy Father's way?—

So, a little Child, come down
And hear a child's tongue like Thy own;

Take me by the hand and walk,
And listen to my baby-talk.
To Thy Father show my prayer
(He will look, Thou art so fair),
And say: "O Father, I, Thy Son,
Bring the prayer of a little one."

And He will smile, that children's tongue
Has not changed since Thou wast young!

ECCLESIASTICAL BALLADS

I

THE VETERAN OF HEAVEN

O CAPTAIN of the wars, whence won Ye so great
scars?
  In what fight did Ye smite, and what manner was
    the foe?
Was it on a day of rout they compassed Thee about,
  Or gat Ye these adornings when Ye wrought their
    overthrow?

" 'Twas on a day of rout they girded Me about,
  They wounded all My brow, and they smote Me
    through the side:
My hand held no sword when I met their armèd horde,
  And the conqueror fell down, and the Conquered
    bruised his pride."

What is this, unheard before, that the Unarmed makes
    war,
  And the Slain hath the gain, and the Victor hath the
    rout?
What wars, then, are these, and what the enemies,

Strange Chief, with the scars of Thy conquest
   trenched about?

"The Prince I drave forth held the Mount of the North,
   Girt with the guards of flame that roll round the pole.
I drave him with My wars from all his fortress-stars,
   And the sea of death divided that My march might
      strike its goal.

"In the keep of Northern Guard, many a great dæmo-
      nian sword
   Burns as it turns round the Mount occult, apart:
There is given him power and place still for some cer-
      tain days,
   And his name would turn the Sun's blood back upon
      its heart."

What is *Thy* Name? Oh, show!—"My Name ye may
      not know;
   'Tis a going forth with banners, and a baring of
      much swords:
But My titles that are high, are they not upon My
      thigh?
   'King of Kings!' are the words, 'Lord of Lords!';
   It is written 'King of Kings, Lord of Lords.' "

II

LILIUM REGIS

O LILY of the King! low lies thy silver wing,
  And long has been the hour of thine unqueening;
And thy scent of Paradise on the night-wind spills its
    sighs,
  Nor any take the secrets of its meaning.
O Lily of the King! I speak a heavy thing,
  O patience, most sorrowful of daughters!
Lo, the hour is at hand for the troubling of the land,
  And red shall be the breaking of the waters.

Sit fast upon thy stalk, when the blast shall with thee
    talk,
  With the mercies of the King for thine awning;
And the just understand that thine hour is at hand,
  Thine hour at hand with power in the dawning.
When the nations lie in blood, and their kings a broken
    brood,
  Look up, O most sorrowful of daughters!
Lift up thy head and hark what sounds are in the dark,
  For His feet are coming to thee on the waters!

O Lily of the King! I shall not see, that sing,
    I shall not see the hour of thy queening!
But my Song shall see, and wake like a flower that
      dawn-winds shake,
    And sigh with joy the odours of its meaning.
O Lily of the King, remember then the thing
    That this dead mouth sang; and thy daughters,
As they dance before His way, sing there on the Day
    What I sang when the Night was on the waters!

TO THE ENGLISH MARTYRS

RAIN, rain on Tyburn tree,
   Red rain a-falling;
Dew, dew on Tyburn tree,
Red dew on Tyburn tree,
And the swart bird a-calling.
The shadow lies on England now
Of the deathly-fruited bough:
Cold and black with malison
Lies between the land and sun;
Putting out the sun, the bough
Shades England now!

The troubled heavens do wan with care,
And burthened with the earth's despair
Shiver a-cold; the starvèd heaven
Has want, with wanting man bereaven.
Blest fruit of the unblest bough,
Aid the land that smote you, now!
That feels the sentence and the curse
Ye died if so ye might reverse.
When God was stolen from out man's mouth,
Stolen was the bread; then hunger and drouth

Went to and fro; began the wail,
Struck root the poor-house and the jail.
Ere cut the dykes, let through that flood,
Ye writ the protest with your blood;
Against this night—wherein our breath
Withers, and the toiled heart perisheth,—
Entered the *caveat* of your death.

Christ, in the form of His true Bride,
Again hung pierced and crucified,
And groaned, "I thirst!" Not still ye stood,—
Ye had your hearts, ye had your blood;
And pouring out the eager cup,—
"The wine is weak, yet, Lord Christ, sup!"
Ah, blest! who bathed the parchèd Vine
With richer than His Cana-wine,
And heard, your most sharp supper past:
"Ye kept the best wine to the last!"

Ah, happy who
That sequestered secret knew,
How sweeter than bee-haunted dells
The blosmy blood of martyrs smells!
Who did upon the scaffold's bed,
The ceremonial steel between you, wed
With God's grave proxy, high and reverend **Death**;

Or felt about your neck, sweetly,
(While the dull horde
Saw but the unrelenting cord)
The Bridegroom's arm, and that long kiss
That kissed away your breath, and claimed you His.
You did, with thrift of holy gain,
Unvenoming the sting of pain,
Hive its sharp heather-honey. Ye
Had sentience of the mystery
To make Abaddon's hookèd wings
Buoy you up to starry things;
Pain of heart, and pain of sense,
Pain the scourge, ye taught to cleanse;
Pain the loss became possessing;
Pain the curse was pain the blessing.
Chains, rack, hunger, solitude—these,
Which did your soul from earth release,
Left it free to rush upon
And merge in its compulsive Sun.
Desolated, bruised, forsaken,
Nothing taking, all things taken,
Lacerated and tormented,
The stifled soul, in naught contented,
On all hands straitened, cribbed, denied,
Can but fetch breath o' the Godward side.
Oh to me, give but to me

That flower of felicity,
Which on your topmost spirit ware
The difficult and snowy air
Of high refusal! and the heat
Of central love which fed with sweet
And holy fire i' the frozen sod
Roots that had ta'en hold on God.
Unwithering youth in you renewed
Those rosy waters of your blood,—
The true *Fons Juventutis;* ye
Pass with conquest that Red Sea,
And stretch out your victorious hand
Over the Fair and Holy Land.

O, by the Church's pondering art
Late set and named upon the chart
Of her divine astronomy,
Though your influence from on high
Long ye shed unnoted! Bright
New cluster in our Northern night,
Cleanse from its pain and undelight
An impotent and tarnished hymn,
Whose marish exhalations dim
Splendours they would transfuse! And thou
Kindle the words which blot thee now,
Over whose sacred corse unhearsed

Europe veiled her face, and cursed
The regal mantle grained in gore
Of genius, freedom, faith, and More!

Ah, happy Fool of Christ, unawed
By familiar sanctities,
You served your Lord at holy ease!
Dear Jester in the Courts of God—
In whose spirit, enchanting yet,
Wisdom and love, together met,
Laughed on each other for content!
That an inward merriment,
An inviolate soul of pleasure,
To your motions taught a measure
All your days; which tyrant king,
Nor bonds, nor any bitter thing
Could embitter or perturb;
No daughter's tears, nor, more acerb,
A daughter's frail declension from
Thy serene example, come
Between thee and thy much content.
Nor could the last sharp argument
Turn thee from thy sweetest folly;
To the keen *accolade* and holy
Thou didst bend low a sprightly knee,
And jest Death out of gravity

As a too sad-visaged friend;
So, jocund, passing to the end
Of thy laughing martyrdom;
And now from travel art gone home
Where, since gain of thee was given,
Surely there is more mirth in heaven!

Thus, in Fisher and in thee,
Arose the purple dynasty,
The anointed Kings of Tyburn tree;
High in act and word each one:
He that spake—and to the sun
Pointed—"I shall shortly be
Above yon fellow." He too, he
No less high of speech and brave,
Whose word was: "Though I shall have
Sharp dinner, yet I trust in Christ
To have a most sweet supper." Priced
Much by men that utterance was
Of the doomed Leonidas,—
Not more exalt than these, which note
Men who thought as Shakespeare wrote.
But more lofty eloquence
Than is writ by poets' pens
Lives in your great deaths: O these
Have more fire than poesies!

And more ardent than all ode,
The pomps and raptures of your blood!
By that blood ye hold in fee
This earth of England; Kings are ye:
And ye have armies—Want, and Cold,
And heavy Judgements manifold
Hung in the unhappy air, and Sins
That the sick gorge to heave begins,
Agonies, and Martyrdoms,
Love, Hope, Desire, and all that comes
From the unwatered soul of man
Gaping on God. These are the van
Of conquest, these obey you; these,
And all the strengths of weaknesses,
That brazen walls disbed. Your hand,
Princes, put forth to the command,
And levy upon the guilty land
Your saving wars; on it go down,
Black beneath God's and heaven's frown;
Your prevalent approaches make
With unsustainable Grace, and take
Captive the land that captived you;
To Christ enslave ye and subdue
Her so bragged freedom: for the crime
She wrought on you in antique time,
Parcel the land among you: reign,

Viceroys to your sweet Suzerain!
Till she shall know
This lesson in her overthrow:
Hardest servitude has he
That's jailed in arrogant liberty;
And freedom, spacious and unflawed,
Who is walled about with God.

TO A SNOWFLAKE

WHAT heart could have thought you?—
      Past our devisal
(O filigree petal!)
Fashioned so purely,
Fragilely, surely,
From what Paradisal
Imagineless metal,
Too costly for cost?
Who hammered you, wrought you,
From argentine vapour?—
"God was my shaper.
Passing surmisal,
He hammered, He wrought me,
From curled silver vapour,
To lust of His mind:—
Thou could'st not have thought me!
So purely, so palely,
Tinily, surely,
Mightily, fraily,
Insculped and embossed,
With His hammer of wind,
And His graver of frost."

TO STARS

YOU, my unrest, and Night's tranquillity,
  Bringers of peace to it, and pang to me:
You that on heaven and on my heart cast fire,
To heaven a purging light, my heart unpurged desire;
Bright juts for foothold to the climbing sight
Which else must slip from the steep infinite;
Reared standards which the sequent centuries
Snatch, each from his forerunner's grasp who dies,
To lead our forlorn hope upon the skies;
Bells that from night's great bell-tower hang in gold,
Whereon God rings His changes manifold;
Meek guides and daughters to the blinded heaven
In Œdipean, remitless wandering driven;
The burning rhetoric, quenchless oratory,
Of the magniloquent and all-suasive sky;
I see and feel you—but to feel and see
How two child-eyes have dulled a firmament for me.

Once did I bring her, hurt upon her bed,
Flowers we had loved together; brought, and said:—
"I plucked them; yester-morn you liked them wild."
And then she laid them on my eyes, and smiled.

And now, poor Stars, your fairness is not fair,
Because I cannot gather it for her;
I cannot sheave you in my arms, and say:—
"See, sweet, you liked these yester-eve; like them for *me*
    to-day!"

She has no care, my Stars, of you or me;
She has no care, we tire her speedily;
She has no care, because she cannot see—
She cannot see, who sees not past her sight.
We are set too high, we tire her with our height:
Her years are small, and ill to strain above.
She may not love us: wherefore keep we love
To her who may not love us—you and I?
And yet you thrill down towards her, even as I,
With all your golden eloquence held in mute.
We may not plead, we may not plead our suit;
Our wingèd love must beat against its bars:
For should she enter once within those guarding bars,
Our love would do her hurt—oh, think of that, my
    Stars!

A HOLLOW WOOD

THIS is the mansion built for me
　By the sweating centuries;
Roofed with intertwinèd tree,
Woofed with green for my princelier ease.
Here I lie with my world about me,
Shadowed off from the world without me,
Even as my thoughts embosom me
From wayside humanity.
And here can only enter who
Delight me—the unpricèd few.
Come you in, and make you cheer,
It draweth toward my banquet-time.
Would you win to my universe,
Your thought must turn in the wards of rhyme.
Loose the chain of linkèd verse,
Stoop your knowledge, and enter here!

Here cushioned ivies you invite
To fall to with appetite.
What for my viands?—Dainty thoughts.
What for my brows?—Forget-me-nots.
What for my feet?—A bath of green.

My servers?—Phantasies unseen.
What shall I find me for feasting dress?—
Your white disusèd childlikeness.
What hid music will laugh to my calls?—
An orgy of mad bird-bacchanals.
Such meat, such music, such coronals!
From the cask which the summer sets aflow
Under the roof of my raftered house,
The birds above, we below,
We carouse as they carouse.
Or have but the ear the ear within,
And you may hear, if you hold you mute,
You may hear by my amulet,
The wind-like keenness of violin,
The enamelled tone of shallow flute,
And the furry richness of clarinet.
These are the things shall make you cheer,
If you will grace my banquet-time.
Would you win to my universe,
Your thought must turn in the wards of rhyme.
Loose the chain of linkèd verse,
Steep your knowledge, and enter here!

TO DAISIES

AH, drops of gold in whitening flame
    Burning, we know your lovely name—
Daisies, that little children pull!
Like all weak things, over the strong
Ye do not know your power for wrong,
And much abuse your feebleness.
Weak maids, with flutter of a dress,
Increase most heavy tyrannies;
And vengeance unto heaven cries
For multiplied injustice of dove-eyes.
Daisies, that little children pull,
As ye are weak, be merciful!
O hide your eyes! they are to me
Beautiful insupportably.
Or be but conscious ye are fair,
And I your loveliness could bear;
But, being fair so without art,
Ye vex the silted memories of my heart!

As a pale ghost yearning stravs
With sundered gaze,
'Mid corporal presences that are

To it impalpable—such a bar
Sets you more distant than the morning-star.
Such wonder is on you, and amaze,
I look and marvel if I be
Indeed the phantom, or are ye?
The light is on your innocence
Which fell from me.
The fields ye still inhabit whence
My world-acquainted treading strays,
The country where I did commence;
And though ye shine to me so near,
So close to gross and visible sense,
Between us lies impassable year on year.
To other time and far-off place
Belongs your beauty: silent thus,
Though to others naught you tell,
To me your ranks are rumorous
Of an ancient miracle.

Vain does my touch your petals graze,
I touch you not; and, though ye blossom here,
Your roots are fast in alienated days.
Ye there are anchored, while Time's stream
Has swept me past them: your white ways
And infantile delights do seem
To look in on me like a face,

Dead and sweet, come back through dream,
With tears, because for old embrace
It has no arms. These hands did toy,
Children, with you when I was child,
And in each other's eyes we smiled:
Not yours, not yours the grievous-fair
Apparelling
With which you wet mine eyes; you wear,
Ah me, the garment of the grace
I wove you when I was a boy;
O mine, and not the year's, your stolen Spring!
And since ye wear it,
Hide your sweet selves! I cannot bear it.
For, when ye break the cloven earth
With your young laughter and endearment,
No blossomy carrillon 'tis of mirth
To me; I see my slaughtered joy
Bursting its cerement.

TO THE SINKING SUN

HOW graciously thou wear'st the yoke
   Of use that does not fail!
The grasses, like an anchored smoke,
   Ride in the bending gale;
This knoll is snowed with blosmy manna,
   And fire-dropt as a seraph's mail.

Here every eye thou stretchest out
   Untarnishable wing,
And marvellously bring'st about
   Newly an olden thing;
Nor ever through like-ordered heaven
   Moves largely thy grave progressing.

Here every eve thou goest down
   Behind the self-same hill,
Nor ever twice alike go'st down
   Behind the self-same hill;
Nor like-ways is one flame-sopped flower
   Possessed with glory past its will.

Not twice alike! I am not blind,
   My sight is live to see;

And yet I do complain of thy
    Weary variety.
O Sun! I ask thee less or more,
    Change not at all, or utterly!

O give me unprevisioned new,
    Or give to change reprieve!
For new in me is olden too,
    That I for sameness grieve.
O flowers! O grasses! be but once
    The grass and flower of yester-eve!

Wonder and sadness are the lot
    Of change: thou yield'st mine eyes
Grief of vicissitude, but not
    Its penetrant surprise.
Immutability mutable
    Burthens my spirit and the skies.

O altered joy, all joyed of yore,
    Plodding in unconned ways!
O grief grieved out, and yet once more
    A dull, new, staled amaze!
I dream, and all was dreamed before,
    Or dream I so? the dreamer says.

FIELD–FLOWER

A PHANTASY

GOD took a fit of Paradise-wind,
  A slip of cœrule weather,
A thought as simple as Himself,
  And ravelled them together.
Unto His eyes He held it there,
To teach it gazing debonair
  With memory of what, perdie,
A God's young innocences were.
His fingers pushed it through the sod—
It came up redolent of God,
Garrulous of the eyes of God
  To all the breezes near it;
Musical of the mouth of God
  To all had ears to hear it;
Mystical with the mirth of God,
  That glow-like did ensphere it.
    And—"Babble! babble! babble!" said,
      "I'll tell the whole world one day!"
    There was no blossom half so glad,
      Since sun of Christ's first Sunday.

A poet took a flaw of pain,
　　A hap of skiey pleasure,
A thought had in his cradle lain,
　　And mingled them in measure.
That chrism he laid upon his eyes,
And lips, and heart, for euphrasies,
　　That he might see, feel, sing, perdie,
The simple things that are the wise.
Beside the flower he held his ways,
And leaned him to it gaze for gaze—
He took its meaning, gaze for gaze,
　　　As baby looks on baby;
Its meaning passed into his gaze,
　　Native as meaning may be;
He rose with all his shining gaze
　　As children's eyes at play be.
　　　And—"Babble! babble! babble!" said,
　　　　"I'll tell the whole world one day!"
　　　There was no poet half so glad,
　　　　Since man grew God that Sunday.

A MAY BURDEN

THROUGH meadow-ways as I did tread,
The corn grew in great lustihead,
And hey! the beeches burgeonèd.
    By Goddès fay, by Goddès fay!
It is the month, the jolly month,
It is the jolly month of May.

God ripe the wines and corn, I say,
And wenches for the marriage-day,
And boys to teach love's comely play.
    By Goddès fay, by Goddès fay!
It is the month, the jolly month,
It is the jolly month of May.

As I went down by lane and lea,
The daisies reddened so, pardie!
"Blushets!" I said, "I well do see,
    By Goddès fay, by Goddès fay!
The thing ye think of in this month,
Heigho! this jolly month of May."

As down I went by rye and oats,
The blossoms smelt of kisses; throats
Of birds turned kisses into notes;
   By Goddès fay, by Goddès fay!
The kiss it is a growing flower,
I trow, this jolly month of May!

God send a mouth to every kiss,
Seeing the blossom of this bliss
By gathering doth grow, certes!
   By Goddès fay, by Goddès fay!
Thy brow-garland pushed all aslant
Tells—but I tell not, wanton May!

JULY FUGITIVE

CAN you tell me where has hid her
   Pretty Maid July?
I would swear one day ago
      She passed by,
I would swear that I do know
      The blue bliss of her eye:
"Tarry, maid, maid," I bid her;
      But she hastened by.

Do you know where she has hid her,
    Maid July?

Yet in truth it needs must be
    The flight of her is old;
Yet in truth it needs must be,
    For her nest, the earth, is cold.
No more in the poolèd Even
    Wade her rosy feet,
Dawn-flakes no more plash from them
    To poppies 'mid the wheat.
She has muddied the day's oozes
    With her petulant feet;
Scared the clouds that floated,
    As sea-birds they were,
Slow on the cœrule
    Lulls of the air,
Lulled on the luminous
    Levels of air:
She has chidden in a pet
    All her stars from her:
Now they wander loose and sigh
    Through the turbid blue,
Now they wander, weep, and cry—
    Yea, and I too—

"Where are you, sweet July,
      Where are you?"
Who hath beheld her footprints,
      Or the pathway she goes?
Tell me, wind, tell me, wheat,
      Which of you knows?
Sleeps she swathed in the flushed Arctic
      Night of the rose?
Or lie her limbs like Alp-glow
      On the lily's snows?
Gales, that are all-visitant,
      Find the runaway;
And for him who findeth her
      (I do charge you say)
I will throw largesse of broom
      Of this summer's mintage,
I will broach a honey-bag
      Of the bee's best vintage.
Breezes, wheat, flowers sweet,
      None of them knows!
How then shall we lure her back
      From the way she goes?
For it were a shameful thing,
      Saw we not this comer
Ere Autumn camp upon the fields
      Red with rout of Summer.

When the bird quits the cage,
        We set the cage outside,
With seed and with water,
        And the door wide,
Haply we may win it so
        Back to abide.
Hang her cage of Earth out
        O'er Heaven's sunward wall,
Its four gates open, winds in watch
        By reinèd cars at all;
Relume in hanging hedgerows
        The rain-quenched blossom,
And roses sob their tears out
        On the gale's warm heaving bosom;
Shake the lilies till their scent
        Over-drip their rims;
That our runaway may see
        We do know her whims:
Sleek the tumbled waters out
        For her travelled limbs;
Strew and smooth blue night thereon:
        There will—O not doubt her!—
The lovely sleepy lady lie,
        —With all her stars about her!

CARMEN GENESIS

I

SING how the uncreated Light
  Moved first upon the deep and night,
    And, at Its *fiat lux,*
Created light unfurled, to be
God's pinions—stirred perpetually
    In flux and in reflux.

From light create, and the vexed ooze,
God shaped to potency and thews
    All things we see, and all
Which lessen, beyond human mark,
Into the spaces Man calls dark
    Because his day is small.

Far-storied, lanterned with the skies,
All Nature, magic-palace-wise,
    Did from the waters come:
The angelic singing-masons knew
How many centuried centuries through
    The awful courses clomb.

The regent light his strong decree
Then laid upon the snarling sea;
   Shook all its wallowing girth
The shaggy brute, and did (for wrath
Low bellowing in its chafèd path)
   Sullen disglut the Earth.

Meanwhile the universal light
Broke itself into bounds; and Night
   And Day were two, yet one:
Dividual splendour did begin
Its procreant task, and, globing, spin
   In moon, and stars, and sun.

With interspheral counterdance
Consenting contraries advance,
   And plan is hid for plan:
In roaring harmonies would burst
The thunder's throat; the heavens, uncurst,
   Restlessly steady ran.

All day Earth waded in the sun,
Free-bosomed; and, when Night begun,
   Spelt in the secret stars.
Day unto Day did utter speech,
Night unto Night the knowledge teach
   Barred in its golden bars.

And, last, Man's self, the little world
Where was Creation's semblance furled,
　　Rose at the linking nod:
For the first world, the moon and sun
Swung orbed. That human second one
　　Was dark, and waited God.

His locks He spread upon the breeze,
His feet He lifted on the seas,
　　Into His worlds He came:
Man made confession: "There is Light!"
And named, while Nature to its height
　　Quailed, the enormous Name.

II

Poet! still, still thou dost rehearse,
In the great *fiat* of thy Verse,
　　Creation's primal plot;
And what thy Maker in the whole
Worked, little maker, in thy soul
　　Thou work'st, and men know not.

Thine intellect, a luminous voice,
Compulsive moved above the noise
　　Of thy still-fluctuous sense;
And Song, a water-child like Earth,

Stands with feet sea-washed, a wild birth
    Amid their subsidence.

Bold copyist! who dost relimn
The traits, in man's gross mind grown dim,
    Of the first Masterpiece—
Re-marking all in thy one Day:—
God give thee Sabbath to repay
    Thy sad work with full peace!

Still Nature, to the clang of doom,
Thy Verse rebeareth in her womb;
    Thou makest all things new,
Elias, when thou comest! yea,
Mak'st straight the intelligential way
    For God to pace into.

His locks perturb man's eddying thought,
His feet man's surgy breast have sought,
    To man, His World, He came;
Man makes confession: "There is Light!"
And names, while Being to its height
    Rocks, the desirèd Name.

God! if not yet the royal siege
Of Thee, my terrible sweet Liege,
　　Hath shook my soul to fall;
If, 'gainst Thy great investment, still
Some broken bands of rebel Will
　　Do man the desperate wall;

Yet, yet, Thy graciousness! I tread,
All quick, through tribes of moving dead—
　　Whose life's a sepulchre
Sealed with the dull stone of a heart
No angel can roll round. I start,
　　Thy secrets lie so bare!

With beautiful importunacy
All things plead, "We are fair!" To me
　　Thy world's a morning haunt,
A bride whose zone no man hath slipt
But I, with baptism still bedript
　　Of the prime water's font.

TO OLIVIA

I FEAR to love thee, Sweet, because
Love's the ambassador of loss;
White flake of childhood, clinging so

To my soiled raiment, thy shy snow
At tenderest touch will shrink and go.
Love me not, delightful child.
My heart, by many snares beguiled,
Has grown timorous and wild.
It would fear thee not at all,
Wert thou not so harmless-small.
Because thy arrows, not yet dire,
Are still unbarbed with destined fire,
I fear thee more than hadst thou stood
Full-panoplied in womanhood.

TO MONICA:
AFTER NINE YEARS

IN the land of flag-lilies,
   Where burst in golden clangours
The joy-bells of the broom,
You were full of willy-nillies,
Pets, and bee-like angers:
Flaming like a dusky poppy,
In a wrathful bloom.

You were full of sweet and sour,
Like a dish of strawberries
Set about with curd.

In your petulant foot was power,
In your wilful innocences,
Your wild and fragrant word.
O, was it you that sweetly spake,
Or I that sweetly heard?

Yellow were the wheat-ways,
The poppies were most red;
And all your meet and feat ways,
Your sudden bee-like snarlings,—
Ah, do you remember,
Darling of the darlings?
Or is it but an ember,
A rusted peal of joy-bells,
Their golden buzzings dead?

Now at one, and now at two.
Swift to pout and swift to woo,
The maid I knew:
Still I see the duskèd tresses—
But the old angers, old caresses?
Still your eyes are autumn thunders,
But where are *you,* child, you?

This your beauty is a script
Writ with pencil brightest-dipt—
Oh, it is the fairest scroll

For a young, departed soul!—
Thus you say:
"Thrice three years ago to-day,
There was one
Shall no more beneath the sun
Darkle, fondle, featly play.
If to think on her be gloom,
Rejoice she has so rich a tomb!"

But there's he—
Ask thou not who it may be!—
That, until Time's boughs are bare,
Shall be unconsoled for her.

DOMUS TUA

A PERFECT woman—Thine be laud!
Her body is a Temple of God.
At Doom-bar dare I make avows:
I have loved the beauty of Thy house.

OF MY FRIEND

THE moonlight cloud of her invisible beauty,
   Shook from the torrent glory of her soul
In aëry spray, hangs round her; love grows duty,
   If you that angel-populous aureole
         Have the glad power to feel;
         As all our longings kneel
To the intense and cherub-wingèd stole
Orbing a painted Saint: and through control
         Of this sweet faint
         Veil, my unguessing Saint
Celestial ministrations sheds which heal.

Now, Friend, short sweet outsweetening sharpest woes!
   In wintry cold a little, little flame—
So much to me that little!—here I close
   This errant song. O pardon its much blame!
         Now my grey day grows bright
         A little ere the night;
Let after-livers who may love my name,
And gauge the price I paid for dear-bought fame,
         Know that at end,
         Pain was well paid, sweet Friend,
Pain was well paid which brought me to your sight.

MARRIAGE IN TWO MOODS

I

LOVE that's loved from day to day
    Loves itself into decay:
He that eats one daily fruit
Shrivels hunger at the root.
Daily pleasure grows a task;
Daily smiles become a mask.
Daily growth of unpruned strength
Expands to feebleness at length.
Daily increase thronging fast
Must devour itself at last.
Daily shining, even content
Would with itself grow discontent;
And the sun's life witnesseth
Daily dying is not death.
So Love loved from day to day
Loves itself into decay.

II

Love to daily uses wed
Shall be sweetly perfected.
Life by repetition grows
Unto its appointed close:

Day to day fulfils one year—
Shall not Love by Love wax dear?
All piles by repetition rise—
Shall not then Love's edifice?
Shall not Love, too, learn his writ,
Like Wisdom, by repeating it?
By the oft-repeated use
All perfections gain their thews;
And so, with daily uses wed,
Love, too, shall be perfected.

ENVOY

GO, songs, for ended is our brief, sweet play;
  Go, children of swift joy and tardy sorrow:
And some are sung, and that was yesterday,
  And some unsung, and that may be to-morrow.

Go forth; and if it be o'er stony way,
  Old joy can lend what newer grief must borrow:
And it was sweet, and that was yesterday,
  And sweet is sweet, though purchasèd with sorrow.

Go, songs, and come not back from your far way:
  And if men ask you why ye smile and sorrow,
Tell them ye grieve, for your hearts know To-day,
  Tell them ye smile, for your eyes know To-morrow.

The Hound of Heaven

and other Poems

FRANCIS THOMPSON

"I fled Him, down the nights and down the days; . . ." A fleeing Man and an ever-seeking, ever-loving God are dramatically presented here in Francis Thompson's best-known work, *The Hound of Heaven*. The deep religious sense of this English poet is expressed in brilliant imagery and sonorous language. Much like the Psalmist of old, Thompson saw God everywhere in the infinity of space, but he also saw a universe in the human soul.

Other meaningful selections by the same author are included in this book.